E220225051

C000064125

I WANT TO BE A

DOCTOR

By Joanna Brundle

BookLife
PUBLISHING

©2020
BookLife Publishing Ltd.
King's Lynn
Norfolk PE30 4LS

A catalogue record for this book is available from the British Library.

ISBN: 978-1-78637-958-0

Written by:
Joanna Brundle

Edited by:
William Anthony

Designed by:
Lydia Williams

PHOTO CREDITS:

Images are courtesy of Shutterstock.com.
With thanks to Getty Images, Thinkstock Photo and iStockphoto.

Front Cover – michaeljung, Stock Up, Anna_leni, ittipon, frantic00, AVA Bitter, optimarc, WoodysPhotos 2 – Monkey Business Images. 3 – VA Bitter, ChaNaWiT. 4 – Alfazet Chronicles, didesign021. 5 – VGstockstudio. 6 – ESB Professional. 7 – Monkey Business Images. 8 – Ljupco Smokovski. 9 – wavebreakmedia. 10 – all_about_people. 11 – Gorodenkoff. 12&13 – Mihail Pustovit. 14 – wavebreakmedia. 15 – Gorodenkoff, ChaNaWiT. 16&17 – George Rudy, BT-Suksan, Viktor Lugovskoy, frantic00, Rido, Lipskiy. 18 – Tana888. 19 – ID1974, Powerofflowers. 20 – Adam Jan Figel. 21 – Michael Leslie. 22&23 – Nata-Lia, imwaltersy, finchfocus, Viktar Kulinka, Dolvalol, Bukhta Yurii, Jiri Perina. Vector Stethoscope: Creative icon styles. Vector Thermometer: Victor Z. Vector Syringe: Sylfida

CONTENTS

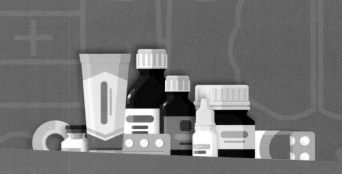

Words that look like
<u>this</u> can be found in the
glossary on page 24.

HELLO, I'M DAISY!

Hello, I'm Daisy! When I grow up, I want to be a doctor. You could be one too! Let's find out what this job will be like.

I want to be a doctor so that I can help people who are poorly or have had an accident. I will be an important part of my <u>community</u>.

People all over the world get poorly, so doctors are needed everywhere.

WHAT WILL I DO?

I will check sick patients to find out why they are poorly.

I will listen to their heart and lungs, and check their ears, eyes and throat to see if everything is working properly.

Doctors must carry out lots of tests and write lots of reports.

Did you know the signs that show someone is unwell are called symptoms?

I will decide what **treatment** is needed and give **prescriptions** for medicines.

I may have to send patients to a different doctor for other tests and treatments.

HOW WILL I HELP PEOPLE?

It can be upsetting and frustrating to be ill. I will help people by explaining what is wrong and making them feel better. I will give them advice to help them stay healthy.

Vegetables and fruit help to keep us healthy.

I will give people <u>vaccinations</u> to stop them from becoming poorly. I may carry out operations or care for people recovering in hospital.

Have you had a vaccination or an operation in hospital? Do you know what it was for?

9

WHERE WILL I WORK?

I may work in a doctor's surgery. This is where patients come if they are feeling unwell. Some surgeries can carry out small operations so that patients don't need to go to hospital.

Doctor's surgeries give special care to patients with conditions such as <u>asthma</u>.

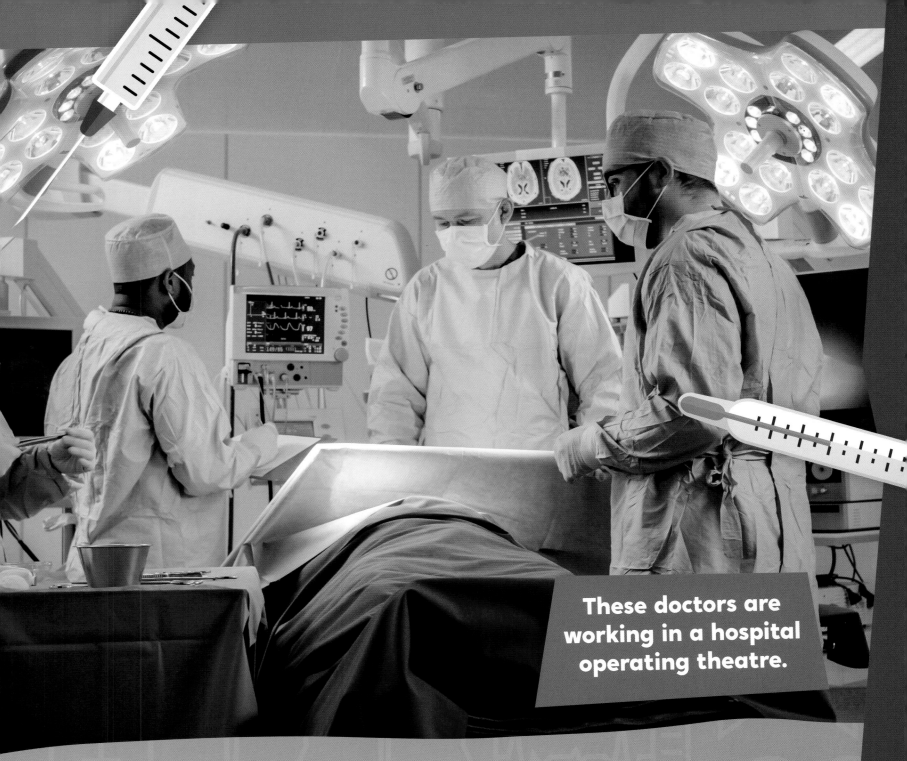

These doctors are working in a hospital operating theatre.

I may work in a hospital. Hospital doctors can look after anyone, from children to elderly people. Specially trained doctors, called <u>surgeons</u>, work in hospital operating theatres.

LET'S LOOK AROUND
A DOCTOR'S SURGERY

The cupboards are used for storing equipment.

The bed is used for checking patients. It can be moved in lots of different directions.

The room must be kept very clean, to stop <u>infection</u>.

Computer

Desk

The sink is used for handwashing before and after checkups.

Chair for doctor

13

WHAT WILL I WEAR?

If I work at a surgery, I will wear my normal smart clothes. If I work in a hospital, I may wear scrubs. Some doctors wear a white coat over the top of normal clothes or scrubs.

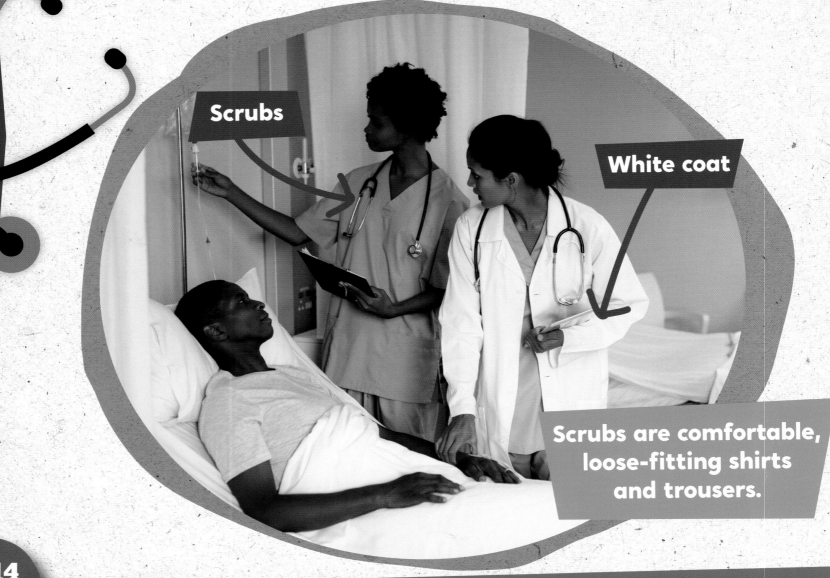

Scrubs

White coat

Scrubs are comfortable, loose-fitting shirts and trousers.

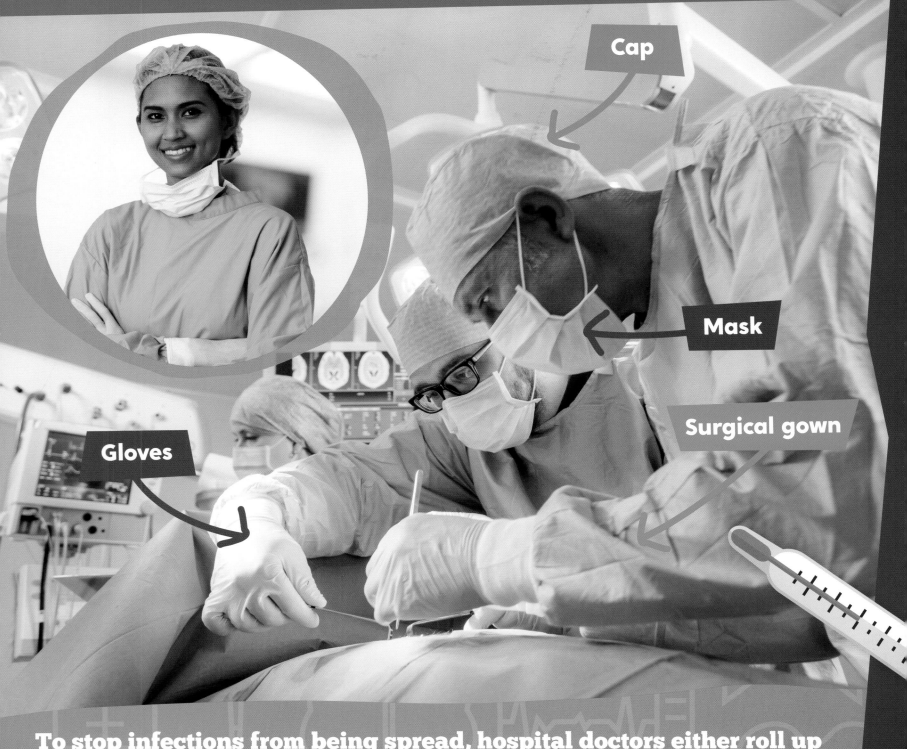

To stop infections from being spread, hospital doctors either roll up their sleeves or wear short-sleeved shirts. In the operating theatre, surgeons wear gloves, masks, surgical gowns and caps.

WHAT EQUIPMENT WILL I USE?

Let's have a look at some of the equipment I might use.

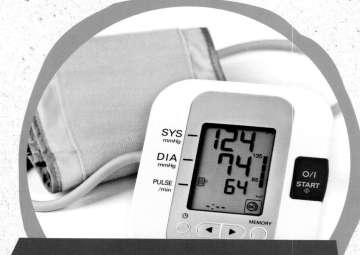

Otoscope – for looking into the ears

Stethoscope – for listening to sounds made by the heart, lungs or tummy

Blood pressure monitor – for checking how well blood is flowing around the body

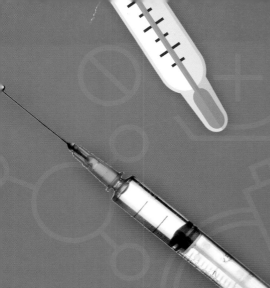

Thermometer – for checking a patient's temperature

Syringe – for injecting medicine into the body

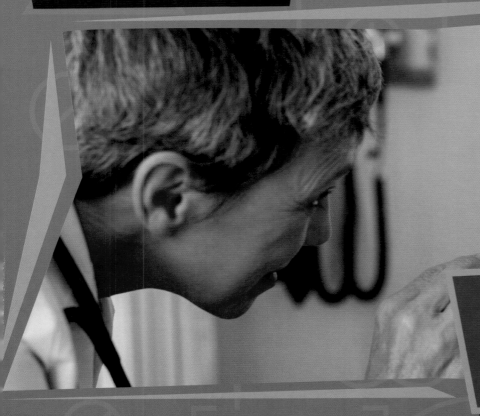

Tongue depressor – for pushing the tongue down so that the mouth and throat can be looked at

17

HOW WILL I TRAVEL AROUND?

When visiting patients at home, I will usually drive my own car. In an <u>emergency</u>, I might travel in a special car called a rapid response car.

Rapid response car

The stripes and flashing lights help these cars to be seen and heard.

If someone has been badly injured and needs help <u>urgently</u>, I may travel to them on an air ambulance. The air ambulance can get the patient to hospital quickly. This could save their life.

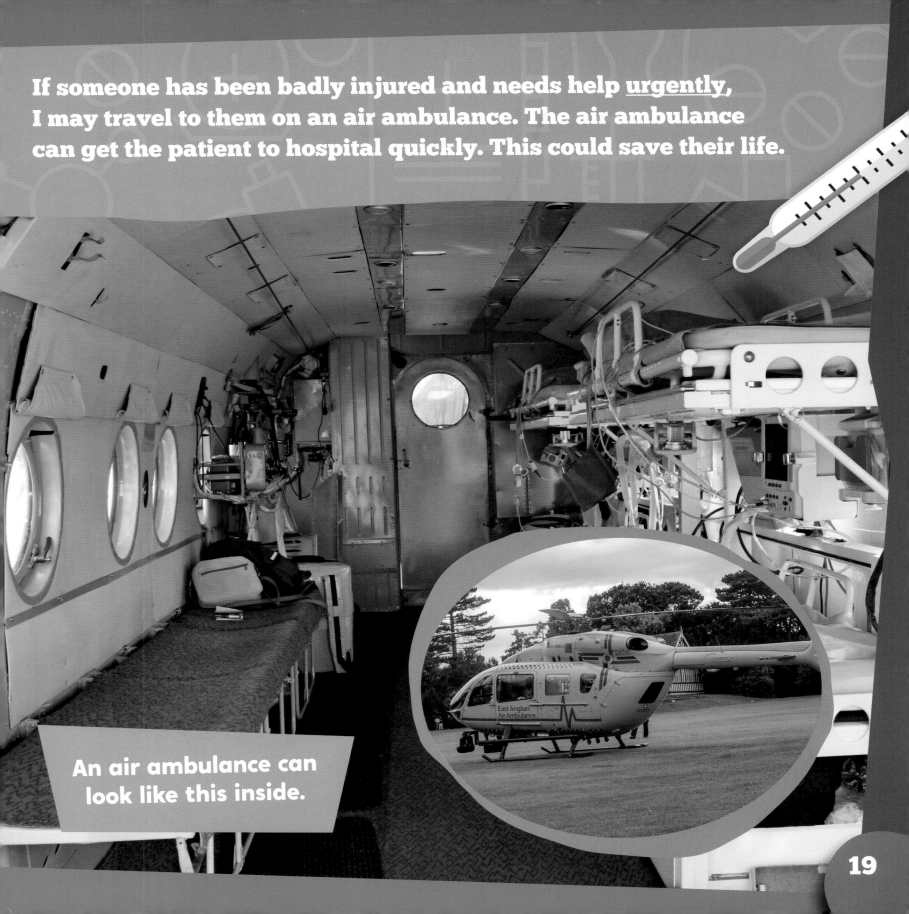

An air ambulance can look like this inside.

WHERE COULD I WORK AROUND THE WORLD?

As well as caring for patients, volunteer doctors help to train new doctors.

This volunteer is working in Uganda.

In many countries around the world, people do not have good access to healthcare. More doctors are urgently needed. I could become a volunteer in one of these countries.

Australia is a huge country and many people live a long way from hospitals and surgeries. I could work for the Royal Flying Doctor Service in Australia, which flies doctors to patients who need help.

Royal Flying Doctor Service aeroplane

LET'S LOOK INSIDE
A DOCTOR'S BAG

I will carry lots of equipment in my bag.

Mobile phone

Glucometer – measures how much sugar is in a patient's blood

To see other equipment in a doctor's bag, turn back to page 16!

22

Medicine

Hand cleaner – for cleaning a doctor's hands before checking a patient

R̸x

PATIENT NAME: _____
ADDRESS: _____

Prescription: _____

Prescription pad – for writing out a person's prescription

Alcohol Pad
70% Isopropyl Alcohol
CE0197
For Disinfection Use

Alcohol Pad
70% Isopropyl Alcohol
CE0197
For Disinfection Use

Cleaning wipes – for cleaning a patient's skin

GLOSSARY

ASTHMA   a condition that causes difficulty with breathing

COMMUNITY   a group of people who live and work together in the same place

EMERGENCY   a dangerous situation that requires action

INFECTION   illness caused by dirt or microbes getting into the body

PATIENTS   people who receive medical care or treatment

PRESCRIPTIONS   special notes written by a doctor which tell a patient what medicines they must collect from a pharmacy

SURGEONS   doctors who work in operating theatres and perform operations

TREATMENT   medicine or other types of care that help cure a disease or heal an injury

URGENTLY   needing action or attention straight away

VACCINATIONS   medicine that is injected into the body to help defend against disease and its spread

VOLUNTEER   a person who works or helps others without being paid

INDEX